ECOCRAFTS

Dream
Bedroom

ECOCRAFTS
Dream
Bedroom

KINGFISHER

BOSTON

KINGFISHER

a Houghton Mifflin Company imprint
222 Berkeley Street
Boston, Massachusetts 02116
www.houghtonmifflinbooks.com

First published in 2007
2 4 6 8 10 9 7 5 3 1

1TR/0107/C&C/MAR(MAR)/128OJIEX-GREEN/C

Author: Rebecca Craig

For Toucan
Editor: Theresa Bebbington
Design: Leah Germann
Additional craft makers: Dawn Brend,
Melanie Williams, Kirsty Neale
Photography art direction: Jane Thomas
Editorial assistant: Hannah Bowen
Photographer: Andy Crawford
Editorial director: Ellen Dupont

For Kingfisher
Editorial manager: Russell Mclean
Coordinating editor: Stephanie Pliakas
Art director: Mike Davis
Senior production controller: Lindsey Scott
DTP coordinator: Catherine Hibbert
DTP operator: Claire Cessford

LIBRARY OF CONGRESS CATALOGING–IN–PUBLICATION DATA
Craig, Rebecca, 1983–
Ecocrafts: Dream bedroom/Rebecca Craig.—
1st ed.
p. cm.
Includes index.
ISBN-13: 978-0-7534-5966-9
1. Handicraft—Juvenile literature.
2. Recycling (Waste, etc.)—Juvenile literature.
3. Interior decoration—Juvenile literature.
4. Bedrooms—Juvenile literature. I. Title.
TT160.C78 2007
747.7'7083—dc22
2006024811

ISBN 978-0-7534-5966-9

Printed in China

**The paper used for the cover and inside pages
is made from 100% recycled post-consumer waste.**

Contents

Ecowise

Turn your bedroom into your own unique space by decorating it with things that you have made yourself. These items will make your room a fun place to be. And they will be special to you— no one else will have the same things as you do.

As well as being really special, all of the projects in this book help the environment by using everyday objects found in your home. A lot of them are things that you would have thrown away. Inside you'll find ways to use an old cardboard box and tubes to make a desk organizer, CD cases to create a picture frame for photos, plastic bags to make flags, and even magazines to make a stool. Recycling helps the planet because it reuses things that would have ended up in the trash.

Around the world, tons of garbage end up in landfills each year. In fact, in 1999 the Fresh

Kills landfill in Staten Island, New York, became the largest human-made structure in the world, overtaking the Great Wall of China. Because air and water cannot reach the garbage buried deep in the landfill, the garbage doesn't decompose, or break down. Even after 30 years you can still read newspapers buried in a landfill!

Sometimes garbage goes to an incinerator, where it is burned. But this isn't a good solution either. The ashes still have to be disposed of—and they can be toxic (poisonous). Burning garbage also creates air pollution. The only really good way to reduce waste is to recycle. For example, by recycling plastic, 50 percent less energy is used than if it was burned in an incinerator. And the plastic can be used to make something else—such as a fleece jacket or even a park bench.

What you can do

Tired of an old toy? Try swapping it with a good friend for another toy. Both you and your friend will be recycling your toys.

Look for toys in garage sales and thrift stores. This way you'll be helping reuse things that would otherwise go to a landfill. And they probably won't come with the packaging that protects new toys.

Bring your old clothes to a thrift store so that they can be reused by someone else.

If you have old books that are now too easy for you, give them to younger friends who will still find them difficult to read.

Pass on old CDs that you no longer like to friends and family members who might enjoy listening to them.

7

ruler

scissors

pen

pencil

paintbrush

tape

paint

glue

Getting started

Before starting a project, make sure that you have everything you need. If you don't know how to trace a picture or make papier-mâché, follow the steps here. Some craft supplies are not supposed to be used by children under 13. If you're not sure if something is safe to use, ask an adult if it's okay. When using craft supplies that have a strong odor, work in a room that has plenty of fresh air. If an object is difficult to cut, ask an adult to help.

TRACING A PICTURE

If you have a pencil, pen, tracing paper, and tape, you can copy any picture you want. The pencil should have soft lead (No. 2)—this will make it easier to do the rubbing over the back. Use a pen with a hard point to make the lines really sharp.

STEP 1

Tape down a sheet of tracing paper over the picture that you want to draw. Using a pen with a hard point, trace the picture onto the tracing paper.

STEP 2

Remove the tracing paper from the picture. Rub a pencil on the back of the tracing paper where you can see the lines that you have drawn.

STEP 3

Tape the paper onto the object where you want the picture to be. Draw over the lines in pen. Remove the tracing paper. The design will be on the object.

MAKING PAPIER-MÂCHÉ

By soaking newspaper in a paste made from flour and water, you can mold and build up many shapes. Use long strips of newspaper when you need to add strength.

Smaller pieces of newspaper are easier for molding. Build up layers until you have the shape that you want. Let the paper dry completely before decorating it.

STEP 1

Measure out one part flour to around two parts water. For example, use one cup of flour and two cups of water. Mix four tablespoons of salt with the flour to prevent the papier-mâché from getting moldy.

STEP 2

Pour the water over the flour. Mix with a wooden spoon until you have a smooth paste without lumps— it should look like thick glue. If it is too thick, add a little more water. If it is too thin, add some more flour.

STEP 3

Rip up some newspaper into strips, following the steps for your project. Dip a strip of newspaper into the paste until it is really soaked. It is now ready to use.

Piggy pennies

You can turn a plastic bottle into a really cool piggy bank that will make a great gift for saving coins. A squeezable ketchup bottle works best.

YOU WILL NEED:

squeezable plastic bottle, scissors, pink paint, paintbrush, bottle corks, black marker, glue, pink pipe cleaner, pencil, pink felt or foam, googly eyes

STEP 1

Make sure that you wash out the insides of the bottle and cap completely. Scrub off the label after soaking the bottle in water. Allow it to dry thoroughly.

STEP 2

Ask an adult to make a hole in the middle of the bottle and then cut a slot large enough for coins to fit through. The cut should be smooth, with no sharp edges.

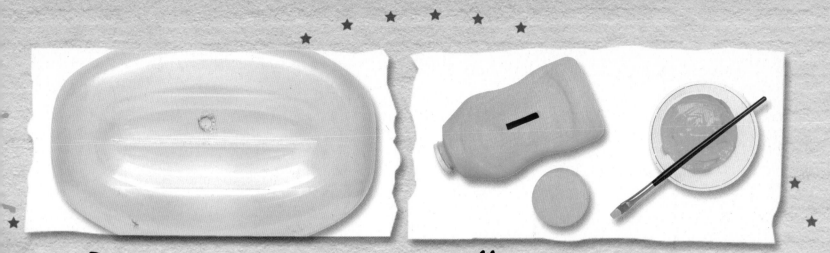

STEP 3

Ask an adult to also make a small hole at the base of the bottle, using scissors.

STEP 4

Paint both the bottle and the bottle cap a bright pink color. Let the paint dry.

STEP 5

If you want short, stubby legs, ask an adult to cut two bottle corks in half. Paint the corks bright pink. Let the paint dry completely.

STEP 6

Using a black marker, carefully draw an outline on each cork for the pig's hoofs and then fill in the outline.

Piggy pennies

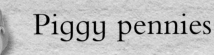

STEP 7

Screw the cap back onto the bottle. Glue the cork legs to the bottom of the bottle.

STEP 8

To make a curly tail, wrap a small piece of a pink pipe cleaner around a pencil.

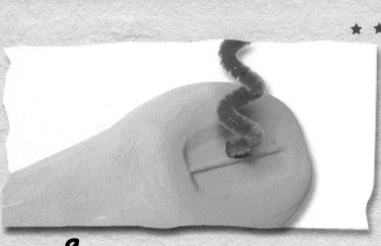

STEP 9

Bend the pipe cleaner to make a small hook at the end of the tail (it will help the tail stay in place). Poke the hooked end into the hole in the base of the bottle.

STEP 10

Using a pair of scissors, cut out two ears from a piece of pink felt or foam.

STEP 11

Glue the ears to the sides of your pig. Try to keep them the same amount of space from the center.

STEP 12

Use the marker to outline and fill in the pig's nostrils. Then glue a pair of googly eyes onto the pig (or draw them in with the marker).

Try changing the ears, tail, and paint color to make a cow or a sheep.

Once your piggy bank is full, take off the cap and spend your savings. Then you can use the bank to start saving money again!

Funky files

This folder holder is the perfect item for storing your magazines, comic books, or homework. You can make it using an old cereal box and some wrapping paper.

YOU WILL NEED:

cereal box, ruler, pen, scissors, paint, paintbrush, wrapping paper, glue

STEP 1

On the front of the cereal box, draw a line from the top corner to the other edge, halfway down. Repeat on the back and then add a line across the side to join the two lines. Cut along these lines to remove the top part of the box.

STEP 2

Paint the inside of your box a bright color. Allow the paint to dry.

STEP 3

Cut a piece of wrapping paper around 2 in. (5cm) longer and wider than the bottom, back, and front of the box.

STEP 4

Glue the long piece of wrapping paper to the box. Fold the edges up at the sides and tuck in the corners neatly.

STEP 5

For the sides, lay the box down on some more paper. Draw a line at the same angle as the top of the box. Repeat with the other side. Cut the paper.

STEP 6

Center the box on the paper and crease the bottom edges of the paper where it will fold for a neat finish. Spread glue on one side of the box and lay the box down on the paper. Then glue the bottom and the other side.

STEP 7

For a final touch at the top of the box, cut a small notch at each corner in order to turn down the paper. Glue and press down the edges.

15

Handy holder

You can make a crafty jewelry holder in the shape of your own hand from papier-mâché! Or make a spooky skeleton hand by painting the hand black and adding some white bones.

YOU WILL NEED:

cardboard, bowl, pen, scissors, tape, flour and water paste, newspaper, paint, paintbrush, glue, glittery shapes (optional)

STEP 1

Place the bowl on the cardboard. Trace around it to make a perfect circle and then cut out the circle. This will be the base.

STEP 2

Trace around your hand, making sure that you include some of your wrist. Cut out the hand and then cut a slit a few inches up the middle of the wrist.

STEP 3

At the slit, bend the wrist in opposite directions to make two flaps. Tape down the flaps of the hand to the round base.

STEP 4

Mix up a flour and water paste (see page 9). Then cut newspaper into strips that are around the width of your finger and around 8 in. (20cm) long.

STEP 5

Soak the strips in the paste. Smooth the strips over the hand and base, making sure to cover them completely.

STEP 6

Scrunch up a sheet of newspaper into a sausage shape and dip it into the paste. Place a "sausage" on each finger to add bulk. Cover the "sausages" with strips of newspaper.

STEP 7

Once the newspaper is completely dry, paint over the hand and base with a solid color. You may need to paint them twice to make the color really strong.

STEP 8

Once the paint is dry, use white and pink paint to make fingernails. When the paint is dry, cover the hand in glue and, if you want, add some glittery shapes.

Once the glue is dry, your handy holder will be ready for some shiny rings and bracelets.

Alien attack

With a few sturdy paper plates (plastic-coated ones are best) and a plastic bowl, you can make your own space station. Before you use them, make sure that the plates and bowl are completely clean and dry.

YOU WILL NEED:

plastic bowl, paper towels, pencil or pen, string, scissors, two paper plates, tape, spray paint, pieces of thin cardboard, tinfoil, glue, tracing paper, colored pencils or crayons (or paint and a paintbrush), paper clip

STEP 1

Use a pencil or pen to make a hole in the center of the bowl. First place a scrunched-up paper towel under the bowl to absorb the shock and then punch a hole with the pencil or pen.

STEP 2

To hang your space station, cut a length of string and poke it through the hole in the bowl.

18

STEP 3

Tie a knot in the string to keep the string from slipping out of the hole.

STEP 4

Tape the two paper plates together around the edges. They will become the rim of the space station.

STEP 5

Center the bowl, upside down, over the top of the paper plates. The string should be coming out from the top of the bowl. Tape the bowl to the plates.

STEP 6

Ask an adult to spray-paint the space station for you, placing a piece of cardboard in front of the string to keep paint off it. Hang up the station to let it dry.

19

Alien attack

STEP 7

Cut out small circles of tinfoil. These will become the windows of the space station. Glue the foil circles, evenly spaced, around the bowl.

STEP 8

To make the alien, trace the template (see page 46) onto a piece of tracing paper. Transfer the alien to a piece of thin cardboard (see page 8).

STEP 9

Color in your alien, using colored pencils or crayons, or paint it. Use as many colors as you want.

STEP 10

Once the alien is decorated (and the paint is dry), cut it out. A simple shape is fine. (If you are really good at using scissors, you can cut closer around the alien.)

STEP 11

Tape a paper clip to the back of the alien.
Then slip the paper clip onto the string
holding your space station.

Hang your space station in your room, using the
string. If you want, try making another space
station using a plastic container, such as
a yogurt container, and make
the windows using caps from
soda bottles.

You can slide your alien up and down on the string whenever you want.

21

Buried treasure

Make a treasure chest to store all of your favorite secret trinkets! You will need a cardboard box such as a shoebox. One without an attached top is best so that you won't have to remove it.

YOU WILL NEED:

cardboard box, cardboard, black marker, scissors, poster board, masking tape, flour and water paste, newspaper, sandpaper, paint, paintbrush, wire or string, ribbon, glue, candy wrappers

STEP 1

To make a lid for the chest, place the box on a larger piece of cardboard and trace around it. Cut carefully along the outline, making sure that you have straight edges.

STEP 2

Cut a piece of poster board the same length as the "lid" in Step 1, but make it 2 in. (5cm) wider.

STEP 3

Tape the poster board onto the cardboard lid along one side only.

STEP 4

Gently bend over the poster board to make an arch and then tape the other side to the cardboard.

STEP 5

To make the end sections, stand your lid on some poster board and trace around the ends of the lid.

STEP 6

Carefully cut out the two end sections.

STEP 7

Now tape the two end sections to your lid. Don't worry if there are gaps, as these will be covered.

STEP 8

Make a flour and water paste (see page 9) and cut up some strips of newspaper. Soak the newspaper in the paste and cover the box and lid with a layer of newspaper. Allow the newspaper to dry.

STEP 9

Using fine sandpaper, gently rub down your box and lid. This will give the box a textured finish.

Buried treasure

STEP 10

Paint the outside of your box and lid a solid color such as gold or another bright color. Allow the paint to dry and then paint the inside of the box a contrasting color such as red.

STEP 11

Paint an edge around the box, two stripes, and rectangles on the sides for the handles. Paint a framed edge and stripes on the lid. Once the paint is dry, make "studs" with the black marker.

STEP 12

Ask an adult to make two holes for each handle. Form a "C" shape out of some wire, bend the ends, and poke them through the holes. Push the ends down; cover with tape.

STEP 13

Put the lid on the box. Cut two pieces of ribbon, the same color as your stripes, around 4 in. (10cm) long. Glue these over the stripes, centered between the lid and box. These will act as the hinges for your lid.

STEP 14

Cut out round-shaped "jewels" from some colorful candy wrappers.

STEP 15

Glue the jewels along the stripes. For the final touch, paint a rectangle on the box where you would like a keyhole. Once the paint is dry, use the black marker to draw a keyhole.

This treasure chest is great for storing real treasures such as your favorite jewelry.

Instead of wire, you can use string for the handles.

In the jungle

A cardboard box, some paper-towel rolls, and a jar lid can be turned into an exotic jungle desk organizer. It's perfect for holding all of your pens, pencils, and paper clips.

YOU WILL NEED:
cardboard box, black marker, scissors, paint, paintbrush, jar lid, cardboard tubes (from paper towels or wrapping paper), colored paper, tissue paper, glue

STEP 1
Cut out the corner of a cardboard box. Draw the outline of some bushes and a palm tree. You can follow the lines in the picture above—they don't need to be exact.

STEP 2
Cut around your outline, using a pair of scissors. Be careful when cutting into the corners.

STEP 3

Paint the base color of the grass, leaves, and tree, using different shades of green and some brown. Let the paint dry completely.

STEP 4

Add details to your tree, painting in the branches. Then add details to the grass and bushes. You can paint in a tiger or other animal if you want.

STEP 5

Cut the cardboard tubes into different lengths. Paint them a bright color inside and green on the outside. Then paint the inside of a jar lid and its rim green. Allow the paint to dry.

STEP 6

Paint some tall leaves onto the tubes, along with some flowers. You can paint eyes for an animal that is hiding behind some of the leaves.

In the jungle

STEP 7

Draw the outline of a parrot onto a piece of cardboard left over from your box. You can follow the outline used in the picture above. Don't worry if it is not exactly the same. Cut out the parrot along your outline.

STEP 8

Paint the parrot, using one color at a time. Make sure that the paint is dry before adding another color. Once the paint is dry, use the black marker to draw an eye.

STEP 9

Cut out several flowers from colored paper. You can use three or four different colors to make your desk organizer really colorful.

STEP 10

Scrunch up some little balls of tissue paper and glue them to the center of the flowers. Let the glue dry and then glue your flowers to the base of the desk organizer—make sure that they won't be in the way of the tubes and lid.

Arrange all of your pieces before you glue them in place in order to make sure that you like the way they look.

As a final step, glue the parrot onto a leaf of the palm tree and the cardboard tubes and jar lid to the base. Your desk organizer is now ready to be filled.

Picture this

Make a display cube out of old CD cases to show off your fabulous photos or pictures. You'll be able to frame five of your favorites at the same time.

YOU WILL NEED:
....
five CD cases, pen, Styrofoam packaging, scissors, glue, paintbrush, ruler, photographs or pictures

STEP 1
You only need the clear outer part of the CD cases, so take them apart—but be careful not to crack them.

STEP 2
Trace around one case onto a thin piece of Styrofoam packaging and cut it out with scissors.

STEP 3
Cut a second piece of Styrofoam, as in Step 2. Glue the two pieces together, one exactly on top of the other.

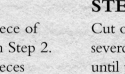

STEP 4
Cut out and glue together several pieces of Styrofoam until you have a block that is the same height as the CD case.

STEP 5

Measure the case with a ruler and cut a photo to the same size. Test the fit of the photo in the case.

STEP 6

Trace around the first photo onto the back of the other photos. Cut the photos with scissors.

STEP 7

Glue the CD cases to the sides and top of the Styrofoam cube. Allow the glue to dry.

STEP 8

Once the glue is dry, you can slip a photo inside each CD case.

If you get bored with a photo, use the gap at the end of the CD case to take it out and replace it with a new favorite.

You can try filling the CDs with dried leaves or pressed flowers.

31

Green fingers

You can make your own cactus using cardboard tubes and a plastic bowl. This cactus does not need to be watered—and it won't have thorns to prick you!

YOU WILL NEED:
....
plastic bowl or container, two cardboard tubes (from paper towels or wrapping paper), scissors, tape, flour and water paste, newspaper, paint, paintbrush

STEP 1
To make the flowerpot, cut the rim off your bowl if it has one.

STEP 2
Cut a cardboard tube into two pieces, with one section a little longer than the other.

STEP 3
Cut the two pieces diagonally at the top. This will allow you to attach the "arms" of the cactus at an angle. Save one leftover piece.

STEP 4
Tape another cardboard tube to the inside of the bowl and add the leftover piece to the top. Tape the "arms" onto the body of the cactus at an angle.

STEP **5**

Mix up a flour and water paste (see page 9) and tear up strips of newspaper. Soak the paper in the paste and start covering the tubes.

STEP **6**

To make spines on your cactus, scrunch up a sheet of newspaper into a long shape. Paste it to the side of the cactus. Repeat this three or four times.

STEP **7**

Paint a coat of paint on the cactus and pot. You might need a few coats so that the newspaper does not show through. Let the paint dry between coats.

STEP **8**

Once the last coat of paint is dry, mix up a darker color and carefully paint the spines to make them stand out.

You can also use a real flowerpot to show off your cool cactus.

In or out?

You can make your own personal door hanger from a cereal box to tell people when you are in your bedroom and when you have gone out.

YOU WILL NEED:
· ·
tracing paper, pen or pencil, scissors, thin cardboard, paint, paintbrushes, plastic bottle, glue, googly eyes

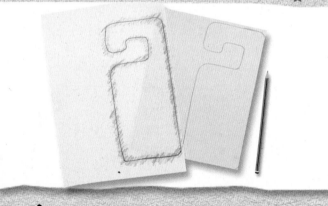

STEP 1

Use the template (see page 47) to trace the shape of the door hanger. Transfer the outline to a piece of thin cardboard (see page 8).

STEP 2

Using a pair of scissors, cut out the door hanger. Try to cut it out as neatly as you can.

STEP 3

Carefully draw a simple flower at the bottom of the hanger. Start with a circle in the center and then draw one petal at a time. Finish with the stem.

STEP 4

Paint the background color around the flower. Allow the paint to dry.

STEP 5

Paint the flower. A bright color, such as red, will make the petals really stand out. Don't forget to paint the center of the flower and the stem. Let the paint dry.

STEP 6

Trace the bumblebee from the template (see page 46). Transfer the tracing to a piece of thin cardboard and cut out the outline of the bee.

In or out?

STEP 7

Paint the black areas of the bee: the stripes, the legs, and the head. Don't paint in the eyes—so you will know where to glue them on later. Let the paint dry.

STEP 8

Paint the yellow stripes. While the paint is wet, use a thinner paintbrush to make streaks so that the bee looks fuzzy.

STEP 9

When the paint is dry, glue the bee onto the flower. Cut out two wings from a plastic bottle. Glue them onto the bee.

STEP 10

As a final touch, glue a pair of googly eyes onto your bumblebee.

Paint a flying bee on the other side of the hanger and then write a different message on each side. Use one message to let your family know when you are in and the other to say when you have gone out.

Buzzed off!

Bee-ing in!

Fly your flag

You can turn your bed into a fairy-tale palace or a castle for knights by decorating it with these flags made from plastic shopping bags.

YOU WILL NEED:

plastic shopping bags, tape, pen, scissors, two bowls, ruler, straws

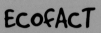

STEP 1
To make a triangle, fold over the top corner on the handle-free end of a plastic bag. Tape it down.

STEP 2
Fold over the other side of the bag to form a point in the center of the bag. Tape it down.

STEP 3
Using a bag that is a different color, trace around a bowl to make a circle. Cut it out.

STEP 4
Trace around a smaller bowl onto a bag that is a third color and then cut it out.

STEP 5

Tape the circle shapes onto the triangle-shaped base of the flag.

STEP 6

Cut out a strip from another bag. Lay it across the flag. Use a ruler and pen to mark the ends and then cut them off.

STEP 7

Tape the strip to the flag. Repeat Steps 6 and 7 until you have as many strips as you want.

STEP 8

Tape two straws together and push them through the handles of your flag.

STEP 9

Tape the handles onto the straws. Your flag is ready to be waved.

Attach a stick to the straws to make your flag fly higher.

39

Bag it up

Why not try making a cheerful wall organizer from some small brown paper bags? It will be perfect for storing small toys, hair clips and scrunchies, or even some letter-writing supplies.

ECOFACT

Making paper bags creates 70 percent more air pollution and 50 times more water pollution than making plastic bags. Recycling paper bags also requires more energy than the energy needed to recycle plastic bags.

YOU WILL NEED:

small paper bags, sturdy cardboard, craft paper, glue, paintbrushes, scissors, pen, small bowl, large bowl or plate, quarter, fake jewels, colored paper, paint, string, strong tape

STEP 1

Decide how many bags you want for your wall organizer. Choose a piece of sturdy cardboard that will be large enough to fit them all.

STEP 2

Spread some glue over the back of a sheet of craft paper that has been cut to the same size as the cardboard. Glue the paper to the cardboard, smoothing out any bubbles.

STEP 3

Use a small bowl to trace three circles onto another piece of craft paper. Cut these out with a pair of scissors.

STEP 4

Trace larger circles onto a piece of different colored craft paper by using a larger bowl or a plate and smaller circles on a third color by using a quarter. Cut these out with a pair of scissors.

STEP 5

Glue the circles together, with the largest on the bottom and the smallest on top. Glue the circles onto a bag.

Bag it up

STEP 6

Glue some fake jewels along the handle and on the small paper circles. Decorate the other bags with pieces of colored paper cut into different shapes such as hearts, moons, and butterflies. Or paint on a pattern such as an arrow or a flower. Glue jewels on them, too.

STEP 7

Spread dabs of glue on the back of one bag. Press the bag down on top of the cardboard backing.

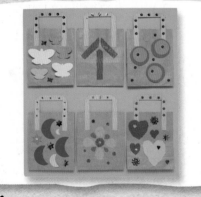

STEP 8

Continue gluing the bags onto the cardboad backing until they are all in place.

STEP 9

Cut a piece of string and form a loop. Tape it to the back of the cardboard with strong tape. Make sure that the loop is centered along the top edge of the backing.

Your wall organizer is ready to be hung on a wall and filled. If you want to put heavier items inside the bags, tape extra loops at the top corners of the wall organizer.

43

Take a seat

You can turn old comic books, magazines, or newspapers into a cool stool. You'll need around 40 of these things, as well as a large container to use as a mold.

YOU WILL NEED:

magazines or comic books, rubber bands or string, large cooking pot or container, old belt, cardboard, marker, scissors, old shirt or other clothing, chalk, masking tape, glue

STEP 1

Roll up each magazine neatly and tie it up with a rubber band or a piece of string.

STEP 2

Place your rolled-up magazines inside a large pot or container, one by one.

STEP 3

Continue filling up the pot or container until it is full. Make sure that the tops of the magazines are at the same height.

STEP 4

Fasten an old belt around the magazines and then remove them from the pot. If necessary, slide the belt down to the middle of the magazines and then tighten it.

STEP 5

Place the magazines over a piece of cardboard. Trace a circle around them and then cut out the circle with a pair of scissors.

STEP 6

Place the cardboard circle on an old shirt and trace around it, using a piece of chalk. Cut out a circle that is 1 in. (2.5cm) larger than the cardboard circle.

STEP 7

Place the cardboard circle in the middle of the fabric circle. Cut notches of fabric every 2 in. (5cm) and tape down the flaps.

Glue the fabric-covered circle onto the top of the magazines. It will make a comfortable seat for your stool.

This makes a great stool or footrest for you or your friends.

Alien template
(for pages 18–21)

Bee template
(for pages 34–37)

Hanger template
(for pages 34–37)

47

Index